TANA HOBAN

I Read Signs

SCHOLASTIC INC.

New York Toronto London Auckland Sydney

This one
is for
all my
children

*With many thanks
to all the sign-finders*

Copyright © 1983 by Tana Hoban.
All rights reserved. Published by Scholastic Inc., 555 Broadway,
New York, NY 10012, by arrangement with Greenwillow Books,
a division of William Morrow & Company, Inc.
Printed in the U.S.A.
ISBN   0-590-48659-4

13 14 15 16 17 18 19 20   14   6/0 5 4 3

3

6

NO STANDING

EXPRESS

DEPT OF TRANSPORTATION

32